GREAT ARTISTS COLLECTION

Five centuries of great art in full colour

MICHELANGELO

by E. H. RAMSDEN

ENCYCLOPAEDIA BRITANNICA : LONDON

Volume seventeen

COVER: Detail from the frescoes in the Sistine Chapel (*see Plates 16 and 17*)

© 1971 by Phaidon Press Limited, London

This revised edition published in 1972
by Encyclopaedia Britannica International Limited, London

ISBN 0 85229 117 5

Printed in Great Britain

MICHELANGELO

AMONG THE SUPREME ARTISTS of the world, Michelangelo, perhaps to a greater extent than all others, became, and remained throughout his life the victim of his own genius. Owing partly to the peculiarities of his temperament and partly to the exigencies of the period in which he lived, he found himself continually disappointed of his hopes and perpetually frustrated in almost everything he sought to accomplish. Yet while in one sense he may have been justified when he said that 'the times are very unfavourable to our arts', in another he was not; since only in an age in which men thought on the heroic scale of the High Renaissance would projects commensurate with his powers have been available to him. The real difficulty, from the point of view of the artist whose goal was invariably perfection, lay in the conditions of patronage which then prevailed. To the painter or sculptor of lesser abilities who kept a *bottega* and sold his services like any other craftsman they hardly applied, but for those more richly endowed little freedom of choice remained once their gifts had been recognized and their services had become an object to be desired by the great. And if the commands of princes were scarcely to be disobeyed, how much more imperative were those of the Church when the Pope himself was patron. 'I have served three Popes,' wrote Michelangelo in 1548, 'but it has been under compulsion.' In all, he was to serve seven Popes before he had run his course, though perhaps not always, nor in the same degree, under compulsion.

Although the greater part of his long life was passed in the service of the Papacy, Michelangelo always remained a simple man at heart. He never aspired to grandeur, but wished to live quietly in his own house and did so, though more of his company would undoubtedly have been welcomed by his patrons, especially after he settled permanently in Rome and became a member of the papal household. That he was generally liked, always respected and often regarded with affection by those whom he served is not in doubt, notwithstanding the reputed *terribilità*, of which Leo X complained. He was certainly irascible, but his bark, as the saying goes, was invariably worse than his bite and his alleged unapproachability more apparent than real. Sensitive and proud, with the heightened nerves of the creative genius, he was exceptionally vulnerable and suffered accordingly. Also, being essentially a man of honour, kind, generous, courteous and considerate (no matter what popular belief may maintain to the contrary), he found it difficult to refuse what was asked of him, whether in small things or in large. To his ultimate chagrin, he was, consequently, apt to undertake more than he could reasonably perform, besides which other commissions not of his seeking were constantly being thrust upon him. When troubled and harassed beyond bearing he became withdrawn and introspective and, on his own telling, was prone to give an impression of being more morose than he actually was. Had it been otherwise and had he not been possessed of a fundamental humanity and a tremendous sense of laughter, he would never have commanded the extraordinary devotion to which the letters of his friends and of those who served him alike bear witness.

By reason of his pre-eminence, and as if to compensate for the epithet 'divine' commonly applied to him, attempts have constantly been made throughout the centuries to belittle him in various ways and to exaggerate his failings. He has, on this account, been as much maligned on the one hand, as inordinately praised on the other, and all-in-all more arrant nonsense has been talked about him, both as an artist and as a man, than can well be believed. 'Oh what a crop of fools these works of mine will produce,' he once remarked to a bishop, as they passed through the Vatican – an observation in which he was better warranted than he supposed.

To pretend that Michelangelo was in any sense superhuman would be to do scant justice to his performance. For it is only when his achievement is assessed in the context of a life lived to an unusual degree amid the fears and temptations, the anxieties and sorrows to which all men are heir, that the magnitude of what he accomplished can ultimately be realized. Again, to imagine with the ignorant that 'it was easy for Michelangelo', would be to misunderstand the whole nature of his experience. Most works of art, as he knew to his cost and did not tire of impressing upon others, are produced only by dint of a great deal of toil and sweat, and by the exercise of inexhaustible patience into the bargain.

It is thus in relation to his personal character and to the historical setting to which he belonged that Michelangelo's prodigious achievement as sculptor and painter (the aspect of his genius with which we are here concerned), as architect and poet must be considered and assessed.

*   *   *

What, then, were his beginnings and whence did he come? From the nature of his descent there could have been no presumption that an artist of any quality would emerge, let alone one who towered like a giant above his fellows, a man for whose services potentates contended and over whom the Florentine Republic itself narrowly escaped going to war. It is therefore small wonder that to this day the little community of Caprese in the Casentino remembers with pride that it was here, on 6th March 1475, that Michelangelo was born. At the time his father, Lodovico Buonarroti, a weak and querulous man, who never forgot, nor allowed others to forget, that he came of a (small) banking family that had known better days, was nearing his term of office as *podestà* of Caprese. At its conclusion he and his wife, Francesca del Sera, returned to Florence, where Michelangelo was brought up, living sometimes in Florence itself and sometimes on the family property at Settignano.

Even during his school days Michelangelo's aptitude for drawing became apparent, and at the age of thirteen he was apprenticed by his father (though very reluctantly, as Lodovico deemed it beneath the dignity of the family) to the painters, Domenico and David Ghirlandaio. He did not remain with them very long, however, but betook himself to the Medici garden to study sculpture under Bertoldo, a former pupil of Donatello's. Here he found a friend and mentor in Lorenzo the Magnificent, who gave him a purple cloak and took him to live in his house, where he often sent for him to show him antique gems and other works of art. As a member of the Medici household he came in contact with some of the most learned Florentines of the day, notably Marsilio Ficino, Angelo Poliziano and other humanists, who had a considerable influence on his thinking in later life.

With Lorenzo's death in 1492 Michelangelo suffered the first blow to his hopes and affections. He was greatly troubled by it and when, two years later, civil strife broke out in Florence under Lorenzo's son and successor, Piero de' Medici, called the Unfortunate, Michelangelo fled to Bologna, where he was befriended by Gianfrancesco Aldovrandini, through whom he obtained a commission to carve an angel for the shrine of S. Domenico in the church of that name, for which he also executed the figures of S. Petronio and S. Proculus, at least in part.

When one considers Michelangelo's *oeuvre* as a whole, one is struck, not so much by its inequalities, since no artist, whatever his calibre, is uniformly excellent, but rather by the unusual dichotomy in his work, which is capable of division into two distinct categories, each of them characterized by features which remain constant throughout. The carvings, paintings and drawings in the one are instinct with those virtues which we associate pre-eminently with the name of Michelangelo – sublimity, grace, profundity and power, in short, all that we mean by that indefinable term, greatness; those in the other are marked by an awkwardness and an opacity that render them oddly incoherent and earth-bound. Indeed, such is the contrast, both in form and content, that it is sometimes difficult to believe that the works comprised in the second group are by one and the same hand as those in the first.

This difference, in manner no less than in feeling, was manifest from the outset and at a time when the disparities could not be blamed upon the inadequacies of assistants, as frequently happened later on. In speaking of the kneeling angel, mentioned above, J. A. Symonds was eloquent in his praises. 'The workmanship surpasses in delicacy all the other figures on the tomb,' he wrote, a statement so patently untrue as to merit but one all-sufficient retort – Rubbish! The handling is clumsy and uncertain and the expression inert to the point of being meaningless, defects that might be expected in a youthful effort, were it not that he had already executed the *Battle of the Centaurs* (Plate 1), a marble relief of astonishing complexity, in which the freedom and the mastery of the born sculptor are already evident.

By this time, moreover, he had also produced the *S. Spirito Crucifix* (Plate 2), a work entirely different in feeling, but of equal quality, which he carved for the Prior of S. Spirito, Niccolò Bichiellini, as a token of gratitude for having been allowed to study anatomy by dissecting dead bodies in a room placed at his disposal in the Convent. According to Vasari, the Crucifix originally hung over the high altar, but it subsequently disappeared and was thought to be lost until February 1963, when it was discovered by Dr. Margaret Lisner in a dark corridor of the Convent for which it was carved. Its discovery constitutes, almost beyond a peradventure, the outstanding artistic event of the century. Though the approach is still tentative, the carving is characterized by an exquisite sensibility and is marked by a tenderness and a restraint that is almost incredible for a boy only seventeen years of age.

Michelangelo's professional career properly began with his arrival in Rome on 25th June 1496. During the four years or so he remained there he executed two contrasted works, the skilful but unpleasing *Bacchus* and the great *Pietà*, *The Madonna della Febbre* in St. Peter's (Plate 4). The latter, a carving of immaculate beauty and consummate accomplishment, in which no trace of youthful inaptitude remains, brought him immediate renown. Elaborately organized in regard both to the pose of the figures and to the arrangement of the drapery, it is replete with a sublime repose. This profound sense of inwardness which it conveys is attributable to the fact that in form as in content the group is peculiarly self-contained. In terms of form it is basically satisfactory, because it can be contained within a compact geometric figure. When viewed from the front it will be seen that the group falls within a circle, the centre of which is the point upon which the gaze of the Madonna is focused; while the circumference is touched at the top by her head, at the base by her robe and at the side by the foot of the Christ. On the left the drapery extends slightly beyond the arc, but this does not affect the central structure. In other words, the group possesses a centre of gravity that is intuitively recognized to be correct. Similarly, in terms of content, the feeling of concentration is absolute, the oblivion of the dead Christ being superbly matched by the absorption of the sorrowing Madonna, in whose contemplation of her Son a moment of time is, as it were, extended into eternity.

When Michelangelo returned to Florence early in 1501 it was as a sculptor of repute and as an acknowledged master. Commissions began to pour in, but few of the contracts into which he entered were ever fulfilled. By the first of these he contracted to carve fifteen figures for the Piccolomini Altar in the Duomo of Siena, but only four were completed and of these four only two are certainly by his hand (Plates 8 and 9). Other works which he undertook at this time include two circular marble reliefs, known as the *Taddei Tondo* and the *Pitti Tondo*, both unfinished, and a circular panel, known as the *Doni Tondo*, one of his three extant easel paintings, the two others being *The*

Entombment and the so-called *Manchester Madonna*, both in the National Gallery in London. An interesting aspect of several of these works, notably of the *Manchester Madonna*, the *Taddei Tondo* (Plate 6), and the *Doni Tondo* as well as of the exquisite *Bruges Madonna* (Plate 5), which was executed at about the same time, is the clear evidence they afford of his intimate understanding and instinctive love of children, who here, as elsewhere are beautifully observed. To this period also belong the *Cascina Cartoon*, destroyed almost certainly in 1515/16, and the *David* (Plate 10), probably the most famous statue in the world.

Then in 1505, when much of what he had undertaken had hardly been begun, Pope Julius II (1503–1513) summoned him to Rome, and, on the advice of his architect, Giuliano da Sangallo, entrusted him with the execution of his tomb, a monument conceived on so stupendous a scale that nothing less than the rebuilding of St. Peter's to accommodate it would suffice. Michelangelo's troubles had begun.

This commission proved to be the great tragedy of his life. 'It is borne in upon me,' he wrote in later life, 'that I lost the whole of my youth chained to this tomb.' For forty years the work dragged on, being constantly interrupted by unsought papal commissions of one kind or another, during which time he was continually harassed by the heirs of Julius, to whom he was irrevocably committed. And when, after many revisions, the monument was finally erected in S. Pietro in Vincoli, it emerged as little more than a travesty of the original design, the *Moses* (Plate 12), which had been all but completed thirty years earlier, being the only figure worthy of Michelangelo's genius. Ironically, moreover, the so-called *Tomb of Julius* was, and has always remained, a cenotaph.

Michelangelo's difficulties began at the outset. No sooner had he quarried some of the marble required and started work, when the Pope changed his mind and announced his intention of spending no more money 'on small stones or on large'. And when, in consternation, Michelangelo sought an audience he was ignominiously turned away from the chamber. This was more than his proud spirit could brook and riding post he crossed the border into Tuscany before the Pope's messengers, who had been sent in pursuit, could catch up with him. He refused to return and a long correspondence between the Papacy and the Florentine Republic ensued. Finally, when war between them seemed imminent, he was persuaded to make his submission to the pontiff, who was then in Bologna. This was not difficult, because it so happened that Julius was far more anxious to placate than to punish him and forthwith ordered him to execute an over-life-sized statue of himself in bronze. Michelangelo, not being a modeller, pleaded his inability to do this, but in vain and, to the admiration and astonishment of the Bolognese, he succeeded in bringing this daunting task to completion. The figure was set up over the great door of S. Petronio early in 1508, but three years later, when the Pope's enemies, the Bentivoglio, regained possession of the city, it was cast down and smashed to pieces.

Although by this time Michelangelo had one or two paintings to his credit, he was primarily a sculptor. 'Painting is not my profession,' he used to say, and this his rivals, notably Bramante and Raphael, well believed. Seeking, therefore, to discredit him in the eyes of Julius, whose known regard for him was the occasion of much jealousy, they prevailed upon the Pope to set him to paint the vault of the Sistine Chapel when he returned to Rome in 1508. Feeling himself unequal to the enterprise and protesting his ignorance of the art of fresco, Michelangelo did everything in his power to renounce the commission in favour of Raphael, but to no avail; Julius remained obdurate and Michelangelo had no option but to obey.

The Sistine Chapel (Plate 16), built by Pope Sixtus IV (1471–1485), uncle of Julius II, is rather more than 130 feet long and 43 feet wide. The ceiling, which at its highest point rises to 68 feet, is 'in the form of a barrel vault resting on lunettes, six to the

6

length and two to the width of the building'. By the beginning of the sixteenth century the walls had already been enriched with frescoes by the foremost painters in Italy, but the vault had been decorated with nothing more appropriate than a spangle of gold stars on a blue background. But what the Pope got when Michelangelo had finished with it was literally more than he bargained for – not what he commissioned, not what he anticipated, and certainly not what he paid for – namely 343 figures for the price of 12.

In a letter written some years later Michelangelo explained the position in regard to the contract in these words: 'Pope Julius set me to paint the vault of Sixtus and we made a bargain for 3,000 ducats. The first design . . . was for 12 Apostles in the lunettes and the usual ornaments to fill the remaining area. After the work was begun . . . I told the Pope that if the Apostles alone were put there, it seemed to me that it would turn out a poor affair. He asked me why. I said "because they themselves were poor". Then he gave me a new commission to do what I liked and said that he would content me.'

'To do what he liked' – the prospect was tremendous: but first of all he had to acquire the art of fresco. This he endeavoured to do with the aid of Francesco Granacci, Jacopo l'Indaco and other painters whom he summoned from Florence to assist him. But to little purpose: none of them was capable of doing what he required, and after a short time he decided to proceed alone, or only with such help as his apprentices could lend him.

Despite much speculation as to the source from which he drew his inspiration, the problem has never been resolved. Vasari, who knew him intimately, makes no mention of a 'programme' based on erudite theological allusions, such as some pundits claim to have discovered in it. Instead, he speaks only of the artistic merits of a work that 'contains every perfection that can be given' and leaves all men 'stupefied'. If, however, a prototype were to be sought, it seems possible that one would need to look no further than the bronze door of the Baptistry in Florence, which Michelangelo himself described as beautiful enough to be the Door of Paradise. It is certain, at least, that in his choice of a programme Michelangelo used the iconographical idiom current in his time and that, in the clarity of its definition, the design for the vault is conceived essentially in terms of sculpture, to which the notion of the niched and socled figure in an architectural setting, both real and simulated, is fundamental. The analogy between the framed reliefs of the door and the four large and five smaller compartments into which the highest section of the vault is divided, as also between the alternating male and female figures bordering the reliefs and the alternating Prophets and Sibyls flanking the compartments, is certainly significant, no matter to what extent Michelangelo may afterwards have enlarged and adapted the theme.

Like Ghiberti's reliefs, these nine compartments are all devoted to Old Testament subjects. Beginning above the altar, the scenes represented in succession are, *The Division of Light from Darkness, The Creation of Sun and Moon* (Plate 18), *The Division of Land and Water* (Plate 19), *The Creation of Adam* (Plate 20), *The Creation of Eve, The Temptation and Expulsion, The Sacrifice of Noah, The Deluge* (Plate 22), and *The Drunkenness of Noah* (Plate 23). Of these nine 'histories', five are reminiscent of Ghiberti's handling of the same subjects, and particularly is this so in the case of *The Drunkenness of Noah*, which becomes the more relevant when one remembers that it was not with the sections above the altar, but with those at the entrance that Michelangelo began his mighty undertaking.

Initially he was far from being satisfied with his progress, as we know from a letter to his father, complaining about his lack of payment, in which he wrote, 'I do not ask for anything, because my work does not seem to me to go ahead in a way to merit it. This is owing to the difficulty of the work and because it is not my profession.' But, as usual, sparing no effort in his search for perfection, he toiled on, always in the utmost discomfort, as he had to stand with his head thrown back in the manner shown in a rough sketch of himself, which accompanies his own sardonic verse –

I'ho già fatto un gozzo in questo stento.
(With this exertion have I grown a goitre.)

In 1510 the first part of the vault was finished and the scaffolding was taken down. In the sixteenth century the marble screen which divides the Chapel stood nearer to the altar than it does today, immediately below *The Creation of Eve*, at the logical line of demarcation between the stories of the Creation and those of the Fall. It was this point that Michelangelo had reached when for the first time he was able to view the work from the ground. Owing partly to this opportunity and partly to the experience he had already gained, he now developed a new style, a style of greater freedom, breadth and nobility, consonant at once with an enlarged understanding of the requirements of the art of fresco and a more exalted vision of his theme.

Apart from the magnificent organization of the design, perhaps the most astonishing feature of the entire work is the way in which a perfect balance is maintained between the unity of the composition as a whole, notwithstanding its complexity, and the elaboration of the parts, notwithstanding their diversity. So that while no component is lacking in its proper exposition, none is obtrusive. Nothing, furthermore, could better exemplify his immense powers of observation and his intuitive grasp of the innermost differences between the young, clear-sighted and active, and the old, purblind and infirm than the variety of age, attitude and expression exhibited by the splendid figures of the seven Prophets and five Sibyls (Plates 24, 25) enthroned with their attendants between the spandrels and at each end. But differentiated though they are as individuals, as a group they are yet united by the intensity of concentration by which each in turn is rapt away into his own inner world.

Again, it would be difficult to imagine a more arresting contrast than that between the glory of God, the Father, the Creator, portrayed in the vault above, and the homeliness of the Ancestors of Christ, depicted in the spandrels and lunettes below – scenes of everyday life, sympathetically observed and simply transcribed with all the tenderness of which Michelangelo was capable.

But of the many elements of which this incomparable fresco is made up, undoubtedly the most daring, perhaps the most beautiful, certainly the most original and the most typical of Michelangelo, is the frieze of the *Ignudi* (Plate 17), who, seated on plinths ranged at intervals along the painted cornices above the thrones of the Prophets and Sibyls hold suspended the bronze medallions which flank the five smaller compartments. In every variety of pose, the embodiment of a strange diversity of mood from the meditative to the turbulent, from the yearning to the gay, these youthful figures, many of whom bear the oak leaves and acorns, the emblem of Pope Julius, all of whom live, immemorially, a peculiar life of their own, are superlative examples of Michelangelo's aesthetic ideal represented in terms of the human body.

Alternately menaced and cajoled by the Pope in his impatience to see the completed vault, Michelangelo was rather more than justified when, as the work drew to its close, he wrote to his brother, Buonarroto, saying, 'I work harder than any man who ever lived. I'm not well and worn out with this enormous labour; and yet I'm patient to attain the end desired.' A month later he wrote again to much the same effect, 'the truth is it's so great a task that I cannot estimate the time within a fortnight. Let it suffice that I shall be home for All Saints – if I do not die in the meantime.' Fortunately he did not die in the meantime, but neither did he return to Florence for the family festival. Instead, he wrote briefly to his father, saying after a short preamble, 'I have finished the chapel I have been painting; the Pope is very well satisfied, but other things have not turned out for me as I'd hoped . . .'

8

On the eve of All Saints 1512 vespers were sung in the Sistine Chapel to mark the completion of the painting. In an entry to this effect in the Diary of Paris de Grassis, the Papal Master of Ceremonies, Michelangelo's name is not recorded.

*   *   *

With the death of Julius II early in 1513 Michelangelo's fortunes changed. During the first three years of the new pontificate he was able to continue his work on the Tomb for the heirs of Julius, with whom he entered into a new contract. But towards the end of 1516, when he had barely completed the *Moses* and the two *Captives* (Plate 14) and part of the architectural framework, he received a commission from the Medici Pope, Leo X (1513–1521), to complete the unfinished façade of S. Lorenzo, the family church of the Medici in Florence. Unfortunately for Michelangelo, as it subsequently transpired, this involved opening up the Tuscan quarries at Pietra Santa and Seravezza, an enterprise on which he wasted three valuable years, only to find at the end of it that his efforts had been to no purpose. The marbles were diverted to other uses, and without any explanation being given, the contract was unexpectedly cancelled on 10th March 1520.

In the meantime he had been working on a private commission, *The Risen Christ*, for the church of S. Maria sopra Minerva in Rome. Though much marred by his assistant, Pietro Urbano, who was sent there to complete it, the work could never have been other than a fiasco, belonging, as it does, to the category of those works which are not recognizably by Michelangelo and would never be attributed to him, if they were undocumented. He himself, as we know, was dissatisfied with it, so much so that he offered to execute another figure in its place.

Whether or not he wished to accept another commission offered him by the Medici towards the end of 1520, namely the completion of the partially constructed New Sacristy at S. Lorenzo, is uncertain. Presumably he did; certainly the execution of the family tombs, required for it, was a project after his own heart. At an early stage of the negotiations he was informed by Leo's cousin, Cardinal Giulio de' Medici, afterwards Clement VII, that 'for these Tombs we should require at least one good piece, that is to say, something by your own hand'. But this, unhappily, was not Michelangelo's way of proceeding nor his notion of the best method of pleasing his patrons. He wished to do a number of good pieces and to carry out most of the work himself. This was his undoing; for unlike Raphael and other masters of the period, he was by nature unsuited to the employment of a large body of assistants and was irked and frustrated by having to organize and supervise work which in the end was by no means always executed to his satisfaction. Moreover, to these petty worries others of a more serious kind were added.

Urged on by an importunate Pope, harried by the irate heirs, hindered by the jealousies of the papal entourage, exasperated by delays in the work and wearied by family disputes besides, Michelangelo had enough to contend with. And then, as if to increase his burdens, Italy was suddenly overtaken by a series of disasters that had a lasting effect upon his career: in 1527 the terrible sack of Rome; in 1528 the outbreak of plague in which he lost his favourite brother, Buonarroto; in 1529/30 the calamitous siege of Florence itself, when all work at S. Lorenzo had to be suspended, in order that he might devote himself to reconstructing the defences of the city.

As soon after the capitulation of the Republic as he was able to do so, he resumed work on the Medici Tombs (Plates 34, 35), but he was ill and dispirited and comparatively little progress was made. So that when he left Florence for good in the autumn of 1534 much of the work in the New Sacristy still remained unfinished, while of the original scheme little more than half had been realized.

Of the projected work only the idealized figures of Lorenzo, Duke of Urbino (1492–1519), and Giuliano, Duke of Nemours (1479–1516), are finished (Plates 36, 37); the semi-recumbent symbolic figures of *Night* and *Day*, *Twilight* and *Dawn* (Plates 38, 39) on the sarcophagi are in various stages of completion, while the *Rivers* intended for the base of the monuments are not even blocked-out. Also, there should have been a sepulchre at the far end, incorporating the twin sarcophagi of Lorenzo the Magnificent (1449–1492) and his brother, Giuliano (1453–1478), with the Medici patron saints, SS. Cosmas and Damian, and the *Madonna and Child* in the central niche above. But except for the two saints, both by assistants, and the *Madonna and Child* (Plate 41) by Michelangelo himself, which is beautifully conceived, but only partially completed, the end wall remains, as he left it, a blank.

In view of the troubles by which Michelangelo was beset during this period of his life, it would have been strange had the melancholy of his mood not been reflected in his sculptures – 'the firstlings of his hand'. So that, if the S. Lorenzo carvings are penetrated by a spiritual unease and a meditative sadness over and above what might be considered appropriate to funerary monuments as such, they do but testify to the profoundness of his disillusionment and to the measure of its sublimation.

To believe with the credulous, as is often done, that Michelangelo's unfinished carvings remain unfinished because he felt under no compulsion to complete them when he had reached a stage sufficient to satisfy his creative impulse, would be to betray a fundamental misunderstanding of the difficulties he encountered and of the conditions under which he laboured. 'Popes do not live long', as Clement VII (1523–1534) was fond of reminding him, and therein lay Michelangelo's misfortune. One pontiff after another, on assuming the tiara, was insistent upon being served and to none were his services to be denied. It is true that the inherent greatness of certain of his carvings is unobscured, notwithstanding their unfinished state, such for example as the *Brutus* (Plate 44), a noble and impressive bust in the Roman tradition, and the *David-Apollo* (Plate 43), whose pose has justly been described as 'one of the most beautiful and graceful Michelangelo ever imagined'. At the same time, it is equally certain that many works remain unfinished simply because, for one reason or another, he was unable to complete them; generally, because he was interrupted; occasionally because he himself became *dissatisfied* in the course of the work.

*   *   *

With the death of Pope Clement on 25th September 1534, two days after his arrival in Rome, Michelangelo lost a patron, who, for all the demands he had made upon him, loved him well. But at any rate he was now released from all commitments to the Medici and free at last, or so he presumed, to fulfil his obligations to the heirs of Julius. But Paul III (1534–1549), the Farnese Pope who succeeded Clement, had other views as to how Michelangelo's unique powers might be best employed, and having long wished to secure the services of the great Florentine, had no intention of being gainsaid, now that he was in a position to command them. He accordingly appointed him chief architect, sculptor and painter to the Vatican, and constrained him, much against his will, to paint the altar wall of the Sistine Chapel. The subject chosen was *The Last Judgement* (Plate 26).

This enormous fresco, which he began in May 1536, contains 314 figures, which create their own pattern and are brilliantly organized. The turmoil is tremendous: in the foreground Charon, an unlikely character introduced from pagan mythology, is depicted with his boat on the river Styx; in the middle air wingless angels sound the last trump; on the left the righteous are drawn up into heaven; on the right sinners are cast down into hell. St. John the Baptist stands above St. Lawrence and St. Peter above

St. Bartholomew, who grasps his skin, impressed with the distorted features of Michelangelo, in one hand, and the peculiarly shaped knife with which he was flayed, in the other (Plate 27). The instruments of the Passion are shown on each side above.

There are two features of the fresco that occasioned immediate comment when it was uncovered on 31st October 1541. The first was the untraditional type of the Christ, who is represented as a somewhat Apollo-like figure, heavily-built, half-sitting, half-standing, shown in an attitude that recalls the question asked of Michelangelo by Pope Julius, when he was engaged on the bronze statue in Bologna, 'Am I blessing or cursing?'. The second, though easier to account for, inasmuch as it has been said of man, 'naked he came forth . . . naked shall he return', caused more of an outcry, since not only the orthodox were shocked by the nudities and, in particular, by the apparent audacity with which the ungirt male figure was ubiquitously introduced.

Though by no means as formidable a task as the painting of the ceiling, the new fresco took him a year longer. But whereas in the past he had been sustained by the élan and the vigour of youth, he was now over sixty years old and, at least physically, past his prime. So that if *The Last Judgement* lacks the inner compulsion, the creative urgency and the inevitability of the vault, who shall wonder? It should, however, be added that we can today have little conception of what its impact must originally have been, before it was spoilt by the ravages of time, the effects of candle-smoke, the efforts of restorers and the meddling of the 'breeches-makers', who added the loin-cloths and other draperies required to counter the scandal caused by the nudities, albeit to the lasting detriment of the composition. We can, however, obtain some idea of what it may once have looked like from a contemporary copy, one tenth of the size, painted by Marcello Venusti for Cardinal Alessandro Farnese, and now in Naples.

Towards the end of his labours Michelangelo probably felt very much as he had depicted himself in the skin of St. Bartholomew. Certainly, he was in no mood at that time to entertain his nephew and nephew-in-law, who proposed to visit him shortly before the fresco was completed. 'It would only add to my vexations, over and above my other anxieties,' he wrote, 'particularly as my assistant is going to Urbino in September and leaving me here alone amid so much vexation . . To have to do the cooking for the two of you would be the last straw.'

Well might he be perturbed and preoccupied, seeing that once again his hopes of being left in peace to complete the *Tomb* were to be disappointed. Scarcely had he finished *The Last Judgement*, when, much against his will, he was prevailed upon by Pope Paul III to undertake the painting of two large frescoes in his newly-built Pauline Chapel. By November 1542 the cartoon for the first was presumably ready, but he himself was so upset by his enforced inability to fulfil his obligations to the heirs of Julius that he had no stomach for the task. He had entered into a new contract with them, but when after three months the ratification had still not arrived he was so mortified that he wrote to a friend saying, 'It would have been better had I been put to making matches in my youth than to be in such a fret', and again in a later letter, 'I am unable to live life at all, much less to paint.'

Yet for all his reluctance to begin, once he had set his hand to the task he characteristically spared no pains in its execution. The walls, as formerly, are crowded with figures in an endless variety of poses; there is no want of dramatic intention in the design nor any lack of invention in the grouping (Plates 28–33). Nevertheless, both compositions betray a certain loss of elasticity of mind, hand and eye and both, to some extent, bear witness to the truth of his own contention that 'fresco is not work for an old man.' Unlike the frescoes in the Sistine, those in the Pauline Chapel do not lend themselves to detailed analysis in the same way. Although they lack the spontaneity and first 'fine frenzy' of the earlier work, each as a whole so far exceeds the sum of its parts as to render it impossible to judge of their impact in reproduction. It is true that some of the figures are out of scale, some of the fleeting gestures fixed and some of the violent movements static, but these are not defects that obtrude themselves upon the beholder when the paintings are seen in actuality. Hence, despite an inevitable fading of the colours and deterioration of the surfaces during the course of the centuries, the Pauline frescoes still bear impressive witness to Michelangelo's innate and commanding genius.

These were his last paintings. During the seven weary years he laboured on them the work was twice interrupted when, to the consternation of the whole of Rome, he appeared to be at the point of death. Happily he recovered, and, spent though he was, continued to seek 'the desired end', until the task at last drew to its close. Then, on 13th October 1549, the old Pope less than a month before his death, mounted a stepladder to inspect the second fresco, which was nearing completion. This second fresco, *The Crucifixion of St. Peter* (Plate 33b), had occupied Michelangelo for 807 days, only two days longer than the first, *The Conversion of St. Paul* (Plate 33a), which he had completed in 1545, the year in which the Tragedy of the Tomb, as it came to be called, was finally brought to a close.

Michelangelo was now seventy-five years of age. But instead of being allowed to rest from his labours, he found himself perpetually encumbered with burdens ever more onerous than before. Already, even before the termination of the work in the Pauline Chapel, he had been compelled, regardless of all his pleading that he was now an old man and that architecture was not his profession, to accept the arduous appointment of architect to St. Peter's. In this capacity for the next seventeen years he served three of the four succeeding Popes, Julius III (1550–1555), Paul IV (1555–1559) and Pius IV (1559–1565), each of whom, after his own fashion, 'not only loved him, but honoured him and held him dear'. Was he not therefore justified in his comment to Vasari that 'those who become the asses of princes early in life lay up for themselves a burden even beyond the grave'?

Though renowned both as a painter and as an architect (having the designs for the New Sacristy and the Laurentian Library in Florence to his credit, and those for the Campidoglio, the fortifications of the Borgo, St. Peter's and other projects in Rome), Michelangelo always remained a sculptor at heart. As he grew older he never ceased to regret that through no fault of his own he had been prevented from following his natural bent. But in the little leisure of his declining years, and especially at night when he was unable to sleep, he once more found in carving his chief pleasure and consolation. Thus, the *Deposition from the Cross* (Plate 46), which he initially intended for his own tomb and the *Rondanini Pietà* (Plate 48), on which he was working within a week of his death, were both undertaken solely to please himself.

For the *Rondanini Pietà*, as we know from Vasari, he re-used a block in which he had previously carved part of another one, of which the fragment of an arm still remains. What his intentions were in regard to it we do not know; perhaps they were not clear even to himself, since it is possible that, as he was wont, he may have worked on it rather as a form of exercise 'to keep him in health' than as a serious project. Its extraordinary pathos and unmistakable quality are not, however, on that account any the less conspicuous.

The great *Deposition from the Cross* belongs to a different category. In this instance we are in the presence of a fully conceived work of art, the impact of which is somehow increased rather than diminished by its unfinished and impaired condition. This is probably due to the dominance of the figure of Nicodemus, in whose features those of Michelangelo are portrayed (Plate 47). At the same time its profoundly moving quality resides in something far deeper than in a mere physical resemblance, since it almost seems as if, in a subtle and indefinable way that is perhaps unique, the soul of the sculptor were here enshrined. Transcended by an infinite compassion, this beautiful supporting figure testifies to the attainment of a state of mind in which the spiritual and artistic strivings of a lifetime have been resolved; to the surrender of a will purged in the classic sense by pity and terror; to a yearning for the divine; and to that ultimate grace of spirit implicit in his own words, 'I serve for the love of God'.

*　　　*　　　*

Architect, sculptor, painter and poet, Michelangelo died in his house in the Macel de' Corvi in Rome on the 18th of February 1564, revered by his patrons, beloved by his friends and universally honoured as the greatest artist in the world.

Outline biography

1475 6th March: Michelangelo born in Caprese, second of the five sons of Lodovico Buonarroti Simoni and Francesca del Sera. Brought up in Florence.

1488 Apprenticed to Domenico Ghirlandaio.

1489 Entered the sculpture school in the Medici Garden under Bertoldo, a pupil of Donatello's.

1490–94 Received into the household of Lorenzo the Magnificent, on whose death in 1492 he returned to his father's house. Studied anatomy. Carved the *Madonna of the Stairs*, the *Battle of the Centaurs*, the Santo Spirito *Crucifix*.

1494 Fled to Bologna during the civic unrest in Florence. Executed an *Angel* and *SS. Petronio* and *Proculus* for the *arca* of S. Domenico.

1496–1501 First sojourn in Rome. Carves the *Bacchus* and the Pietà – the *Madonna della Febbre*.

1501–05 Worked in Florence. Executed the *David*, the *Bruges Madonna*, the Piccolomini Altar figures (in part), the Doni, Pitti and Taddei *Tondi*.

1505 Summoned to Rome by Julius II (1503–1513) and commissioned to execute his Tomb.

1506 Fled from Rome to Florence. Completed the *Cascina Cartoon*. Made his submission to the Pope at Bologna and was ordered to execute his statue in bronze. Completed the work in 1508.

1508–12 Engaged on the painting of the frescoes of the vault of the Sistine Chapel in Rome.

1513–16 Entered into the first and second contracts with the heirs of Julius for the Pope's Tomb. Executed the *Moses* and *Captives* as part of the project.

1516–20 Engaged on the façade of S. Lorenzo in Florence to the order of Leo X (1513–1521). Compelled to open up the marble quarries at Pietrasanta and Seravezza. Contract cancelled 10th March.

1520–28 Engaged on the building of the New Sacristy and the Laurentian Library at S. Lorenzo

and on the Medici Tombs. Executed the *Risen Christ* and continues work on the Tomb of Julius.

1529 Appointed Superintendent of the fortifications in anticipation of the siege of Florence. Painted *Leda and the Swan* during the suspension of the work at S. Lorenzo. Florence invested by the troops of Clement VII (1523–1534) in October.

1530 Capitulation of Florence: fall of the Republic.

1531–33 Resumed work at S. Lorenzo. Entered into a third contract for the Julius Tomb. Executed the *David–Apollo*.

1534 Leaving the work at S. Lorenzo unfinished Michelangelo left Florence for good to live permanently in Rome.

1535 Appointed supreme sculptor, painter and architect to the Vatican by Paul III (1534–1549).

1536–41 Painted *The Last Judgement* in the Sistine Chapel. Worked on designs for the Campidoglio.

1542–45 Fourth and last contract with the heirs of Julius. Painted *The Conversion of St. Paul* in the Pauline Chapel. Completed the Julius Tomb in S. Pietro in Vincoli.

1546 Continued work on *The Crucifixion of St. Peter* in the Pauline Chapel. Received the honour of Roman citizenship.

1547 Appointed architect of St. Peter's Basilica.

1550 Completed *The Crucifixion of St. Peter*.

1551–63 Though pressed by Duke Cosimo to return to Florence, he continued to hold office as architect of St. Peter's under the succeeding Popes: Julius III (1550–1555), Marcellus II (1555), Paul IV (1555–1559) and Pius IV (1559–1565). Also worked on various architectural projects, on *The Deposition from the Cross* and on the *Rondanini Pietà*.

1564 18th February: died in his house in Rome and, after extended obsequies in S. Lorenzo, was buried in the family vault in S. Croce in Florence.

1. *The Battle of the Centaurs.* Marble relief.
33¼ × 35½ in. (84·5 × 90 cm.). 1492. Florence,
Casa Buonarroti.

In conception, this relief, which was originally
known as *The Rape of Deianeira*, owes much to
the influence of Michelangelo's master, Bertoldo
di Giovanni. Compare the bronze relief *Battle
of the Romans and Barbarians* in the Bargello in
Florence.

2. *Head of Christ.* Detail of the *S. Spirito Crucifix*.
Painted wood. Crucifix figure 21¾ × 15¾ in.
(55·5 × 40 cm.). 1493. Florence, Casa Buonarroti.

This is Michelangelo's only finished carving in
wood. Note the difference in the treatment of
the hair from that with which we are familiar in
his carving of marble.

3. *Head of Christ.* Detail of Plate 4.

In his treatment of the head of Christ Michelangelo appears to have had a preference for the
short beard. Compare the S. Spirito Crucifix
(Plate 2) and the painting of *The Entombment*
in the National Gallery, London.

4. *Pietà*, called *Madonna della Febbre*. Marble.
68½ × 76¾ in. (1·74 × 1·95 m.). 1498–9. Rome,
St. Peter's Basilica.

This is the only signed work by Michelangelo.
Having heard it being attributed to another, he
hid in the chapel and carved his name across the
baldric during the night: MICHAEL · ANGELVS ·
BONAROTVS · FLORENT · FACIEBAT.

5. *Madonna and Child*, called *The Bruges Madonna*.
Marble, 50½ in. high (1·28 m.). About 1504.
Bruges, Church of Notre-Dame.

The precise date of its execution is not known.
It was shipped to Flanders in 1506. A singularly
beautiful and eminently sculptural piece.

6. *Madonna and Child*, called *The Taddei Tondo*.
Marble relief. 43 in. (1.09 m.) diameter. About
1504. London, Royal Academy of Arts.

The little St. John holds a goldfinch, a symbol
of the Passion, from which the Child shies away.
A good deal of nonsense has been talked about
the source of its inspiration. It was acquired by
Sir George Beaumont in Rome in 1822 and
later bequeathed to the Royal Academy.

7. *The Christ Child.* Detail of Plate 5.

Compare the carving of the hair which is
characteristic, with the heads in Plates 8 and 9.

8–9. *St. Peter* and *St. Paul.* Statues from the
Piccolomini Altar. Marble, 47¼ in. high (1·20
m.). 1501–4. Siena, Duomo.

The Altar, by Andrea Bregno, stands against the
wall in the north aisle. Some scholars assign the
two figures, St. Gregory and St. Pius, to Michelangelo, who may have supplied the drawings,
but would appear to have had no hand in the
work.

10. *David.* Marble. 14 ft. 3 in. high, including base
(4·34 m.). 1501–4. Florence, Accademia di Belle
Arti.

The block, which had already been partly worked
by Agostino di Duccio, was assigned to Michelangelo by the Commissioners of the Cathedral
in 1501. The statue was erected outside the
Palazzo Vecchio but removed to the Accademia
in 1875 and a copy was set up in the Piazza in its
stead. The left arm, broken in 1527, was
subsequently repaired.

11. *Head of David.* Detail of Plate 10.

The form of the eye, the nose and the mouth
has provided a model for these features in art
schools up to the present day.

12–13. *Moses*, central statue from the Tomb of Pope
Julius II. Marble. 7 ft. 8½ in. high (2·35 m.).
1513–16. Rome, Church of S. Pietro in Vincoli.
The five other figures included in the monument, largely by other hands, are wholly
negligible. Apart from the Moses, only the
arabesques of the architectural frame are characteristic of Michelangelo's work. Moses is
shown with the traditional horns, which
originated from a mistranslation in the Vulgate
of the Hebrew word for 'light' (Exodus 34.29).

14. *The Dying Captive* and *The Rebellious Captive.*
Marble. 7 ft. 6½ in. (2·29 m.) and 7 ft. 1 in.
(2·15 m.). 1513–16. Paris, Louvre.

These figures were originally intended for the
Tomb of Julius, but were deemed unsuitable
when the project was reduced in scale. They
were given by Roberto Strozzi to Henry II of
France. For an account of how Roberto Strozzi
acquired them, see *The Letters of Michelangelo*
by E. H. Ramsden, 1963, Vol. II, p. 244 ff.

15. *The First and Second 'Boboli Captives'.* Marble.
8 ft. 5 in. (2·56 m.) and 9 ft. 1 in. (2·77 m.).
1518–26. Florence, Accademia di Belle Arti.

These half blocked-out figures, intended for the
Tomb of Julius, once stood in the Boboli
Gardens. Hence the name. They are generally
dated about 1530, but this cannot be correct,
owing to Michelangelo's movements after the
siege of Florence.

16. *The Sistine Chapel*, general view. Rome,
Vatican Palace.

The chapel was built for Pope Sixtus IV
(1471–84) by Giovanni de' Dolce and Baccio
Pontelli. The 'histories' on the walls had already
been painted when Michelangelo began work on
the vault, the surface of which, according to
J. A. Symonds, is 10,000 sq. ft. *The Last
Judgment* is seen on the altar wall. In the
sixteenth century the marble screen stood on the
other side of the *cantoria* below the point where
Michelangelo ended the first and began the
second stage of his work on the vault.

17–25. *Frescoes of the Sistine Vault*. Details. See Plate 16.

The frescoes were executed in inverse order to the Biblical narrative. The first part, from the entrance to the marble screen, was painted in 1508–10, the second part, from the screen to the altar, in 1510–12.

17. *Ignudo*.

One of the twenty decorative nudes which flank the five smaller compartments. Some have been damaged and one was destroyed by the blast of an explosion in 1797. The mood and pose of each one is different.

18. *The Creation of the Sun and Moon and of the Plants*.

The first in the order of the narrative of Creation (but the last in the order of execution) of the four larger compartments. Note the commanding gesture of God the Father creating the heavenly bodies and the speed of his movement as he hastens away to create 'the tree giving fruit after its kind'.

19. *The Division of Land and Water*.

The second of the smaller compartments.

20. *The Creation of Adam*.

The second of the larger compartments and the one on which Michelangelo began when the scaffolding was re-erected in its new position in 1510. It is probably the most famous fresco in the world and certainly one of the most beautiful.

21. *The Creation of Adam*. Detail of Plate 20.

The joins between the sections of plaster indicate that Michelangelo painted the whole figure in three days.

22. *The Deluge*. Detail of the fourth of the larger compartments.

The sense of urgency and the dramatic intensity of the moment is marvellously conveyed, while at the same time the numerous domestic details are casually introduced.

23. *The Drunkenness of Noah*.

The last of the smaller compartments in the narrative sequence and the first to be executed. It closely resembles Ghiberti's treatment of the same subject on the bronze door of the Baptistry in Florence.

24. *The Erythrean Sibyl*.

The youngest of the five Sibyls. Note the strangely devised garments and elaborate head-dress. The *putto* behind her is lighting a lamp.

25. *The Prophet Joel*.

One of the seven Prophets who alternate with the five Sibyls in the lateral pendentives. Probably the first of these monumental figures to be painted. Note the concentration with which he peruses his scroll.

26. *The Last Judgement*. Altar wall of the Sistine Chapel. Fresco. 48 × 44 ft. (14·63 × 13·30 m.). 1536–41. Rome, Vatican Palace.

Perhaps mistakenly Michelangelo rejected the idea of framing the composition, which has somewhat the appearance of being suspended in space. There are many anecdotes connected with its execution. See *Michelangelo* by Ludwig Goldscheider, 1963, p. 19 f.

27. *St. Bartholomew*. Detail of Plate 26.

The full significance of Michelangelo's portrayal of his own features in the skin of the saint is not known. Various interpretations have been suggested, but none sufficiently convincing to warrant acceptance. Arguments for identifying the figure of St. Bartholomew with Pietro Aretino, the 'Scourge of Princes', are likewise inconclusive.

28, 31, 32. *The Conversion of St. Paul*. Details of Plate 33a.

Awed by the sight and sound of the heavenly vision, the companions of St. Paul gaze upwards towards the congregation of the Blessed, who look towards the descending figure of Christ. St. Paul, a powerfully rendered figure in the foreground, is, by contrast, blinded by the vision.

29, 30. *The Crucifixion of St. Peter*. Details of Plate 33b.

St. Peter, whose expression is defiant rather than agonized, has been nailed to the cross and the soldiers are exerting themselves to raise it and insert it into the hole that is being dug. The huge, saffron-robed figure on the right, apparently oblivious to what is passing, remains enigmatic.

33a & b. *The Conversion of St. Paul* and *The Crucifixion of St. Peter*. Frescoes. Each 20 ft. 6 in. × 21 ft. 10 in. (6.25 × 6.61 m.). 1542–45 and 1545–50. Rome, Pauline Chapel, Vatican Palace.

Note the range of ages, the variety of expressions and the predilection for back views shown in both frescoes.

34. *Tomb of Lorenzo de' Medici*. Marble. 1524–33. Florence, Medici Chapel, New Sacristy, S. Lorenzo.

The Duke, in Roman dress, is shown seated in a niche above the sarcophagus, on which the symbolic figures of Twilight and Dawn recline.

35. *Tomb of Giuliano de' Medici*. Marble. 1524–33. Florence, Medici Chapel, New Sacristy, S. Lorenzo.

The Duke, likewise in Roman dress, is shown seated in a niche above the sarcophagus, on which the symbolic figures of Night and Day recline.

36. *Lorenzo de' Medici*. Detail of Plate 34. Marble. 5 ft. 10 in. (1·78 m.).

Lorenzo de' Medici, Duke of Urbino (1492–1519), father of Catherine de' Medici, Queen of France. Many theories have been advanced to explain the significance of the closed box with the bat's head, on which he rests his elbow, as of the coins held by the companion figure of Giuliano, but no definite conclusion has been reached.

37. *Giuliano de' Medici.* Detail of Plate 35. Marble. 5 ft. 8 in. (1·73 m.).
Giuliano de' Medici, Duke of Nemours (1499–1516). He is shown with the commander's baton. Both dukes are idealized figures, perhaps fortunately, having regard to the conspicuous lack of good looks in the family. The details of the accoutrements in both cases were executed by assistants.

38. *Twilight.* Detail of Plate 34. Marble. 6 ft. 4¾ in. (1·95 m.).
The feeling of inertia and of languid repose is perfectly conveyed.

39. *Dawn.* Detail of Plate 34. Marble. 6 ft. 8 in. (2·03 m.).
The feeling of rising, however reluctantly, as opposed to the sinking of the Twilight, is again masterly. Perhaps the most tragic of the four symbolic figures.

40. *Owl.* Detail of Plate 35.
A symbol of Night, perched under the raised leg of the sleeping figure. Not particularly characteristic of Michelangelo, it is an unexpected and delightful addition.

41. *Madonna and Child.* Detail of the so-called 'Medici Madonna'. Marble. 7 ft. 5 in. (2·26 m.). 1524–33. Medici Chapel. See Plates 34 and 35.
The expression, as of all the New Sacristy figures, is sad and withdrawn, and the work, like so much else in the chapel, remains unfinished. Here again we see Michelangelo's sympathetic handling of the Child.

42. *Victory.* Marble. 8 ft. 6¾ in. (2·61 m.). Perhaps 1530. Florence, Palazzo Vecchio.
It is not known when, for whom or for what purpose this somewhat unsatisfactory piece was undertaken. The disproportionate head, the treatment of the hair and the exaggerated torso would suggest the intervention of assistants.

43. *David-Apollo.* Marble. 4 ft. 9½ in., including base (1·46 m.). 1531. Florence, Museo Nazionale del Bargello.
There is very little doubt that this singularly fine piece was carved for Baccio Valori, the Pope's representative in Florence, after the siege.

44. *Brutus.* Marble. 37½ in. (95 cm.). 1542–5. Florence, Museo Nazionale del Bargello.
This powerful bust in the Roman tradition is the only work of its kind in Michelangelo's *oeuvre*. The toga is said to have been completed by his assistant, Tiberio Calcagni.

45. *Head of the 'Bearded Captive'.* Detail. Marble. 1518–26. Florence, Accademia di Belle Arti.
Like the other half blocked-out *Captives* it was given to Duke Cosimo I by Michelangelo's nephew Lionardo. Note the vigorous method of the blocking-out and the contrast between the treatment of the face and the hair.

46. *The Deposition from the Cross.* Marble. 7 ft. 5 in. (2·26 m.). 1548–56. Florence, Duomo.
Having discovered a flaw in the marble and made an error in the cutting, Michelangelo began to smash it up, but was dissuaded by his servant. Tiberio Calcagni repaired the broken left arm and right hand of the Christ and spoilt the figure of Mary Magdalene.

47. *Head of Nicodemus.* Detail of Plate 46.
The features are the features of Michelangelo, who designed the group initially as his own memorial.

48. *Rondanini Pietà.* Marble. 6 ft. 4¾ in. (1·95 m.). 1556–64. Milan, Castello Sforzesco.
Michelangelo worked on the group intermittently during the last years of his life. The disproportionate legs of the Christ and the detached arm were originally intended for a group on a larger scale. The group long stood in the courtyard of the Rondanini Palace in Rome and was acquired by the commune of Milan in 1952.

The reproductions of the frescoes in the Pauline Chapel of the Vatican (Plates 28–33) were made from photographs taken with the support of the Samuel H. Kress Foundation, New York.
Colour photographs: Plates 18, 20, 22, 24–7, Scala, Florence; Plates 28–32, Ronald Sheridan, London; Plates 17, 19, 21, 23, Phaidon Press Archives.
Photo Plate 2, Bruno Balestrini-Electa, Milan.

1. *THE BATTLE OF THE CENTAURS*. Marble relief. 1492. Florence, Casa Buonarroti

2. *HEAD OF CHRIST*. Detail of the S. Spirito Crucifix. Painted wood. 1493. Florence, Casa Buonarroti

3. *HEAD OF CHRIST*. Detail of Plate 4

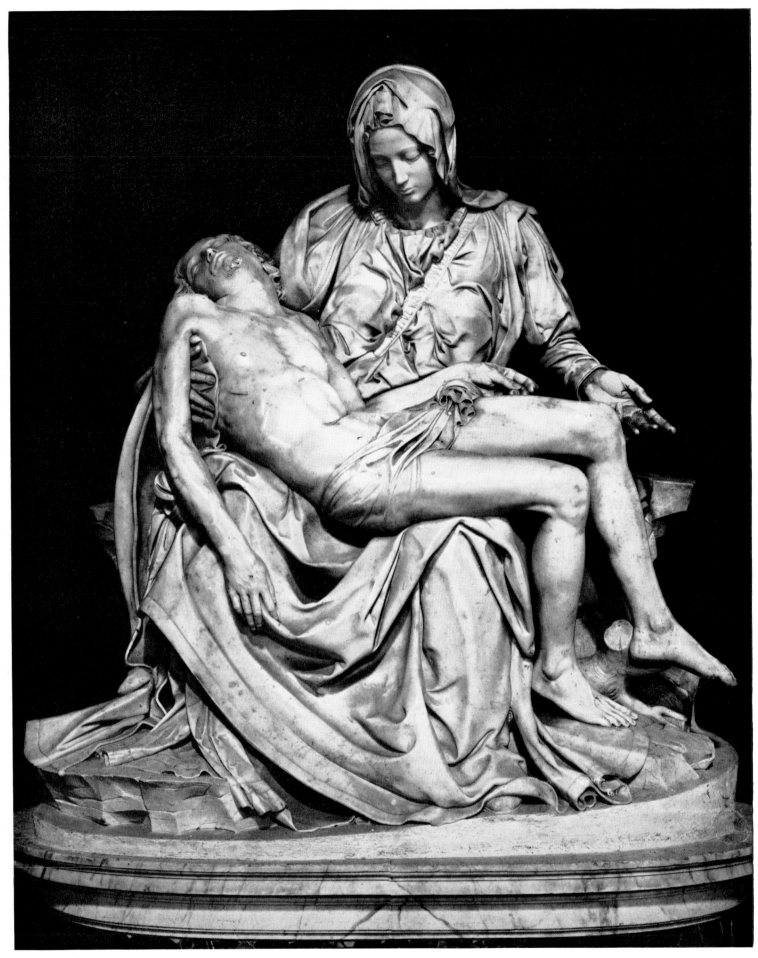

4. *PIETÀ*. Marble. 1498–9. Rome, St. Peter's Basilica

5. *MADONNA AND CHILD* (The Bruges Madonna). Marble.
About 1504. Bruges, Church of Notre-Dame

6. *MADONNA AND CHILD* (The Taddei Tondo). Marble relief. About 1504. London, Royal Academy

7. *THE CHRIST CHILD.* Detail of Plate 5

8. *ST. PETER: ST. PAUL.* Statues from the Piccolomini Altar. Marble. 1501–4. Siena, Duomo

9. *HEAD OF ST. PAUL.* Detail of Plate 8

10. *DAVID*. Marble. 1501–4. Florence, Accademia

11. *HEAD OF DAVID*. Detail of Plate 10

12. *MOSES*. Statue from the Tomb of Pope Julius II. Marble. 1513–16. Rome, S. Pietro in Vincoli

13. *MOSES*. Detail of Plate 12

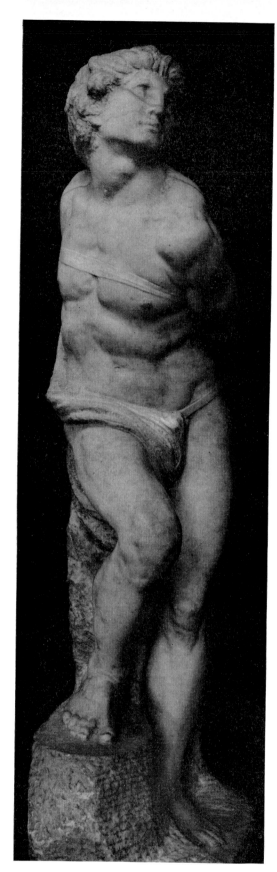

14. *DYING CAPTIVE: REBELLIOUS CAPTIVE.* Marble. About 1513–16. Paris, Louvre

FIRST 'BOBOLI' CAPTIVE: SECOND 'BOBOLI' CAPTIVE. Marble. 1518–26. Florence, Accademia

16. *THE SISTINE CHAPEL.* View showing frescoes of the vault and the altar wall. Rome, Vatican Palace

17. *IGNUDO*. Detail of the vault. 1508–10. Rome, Sistine Chapel

18. *THE CREATION OF SUN AND MOON.* Detail of the vault. 1510–12. Rome, Sistine Chapel

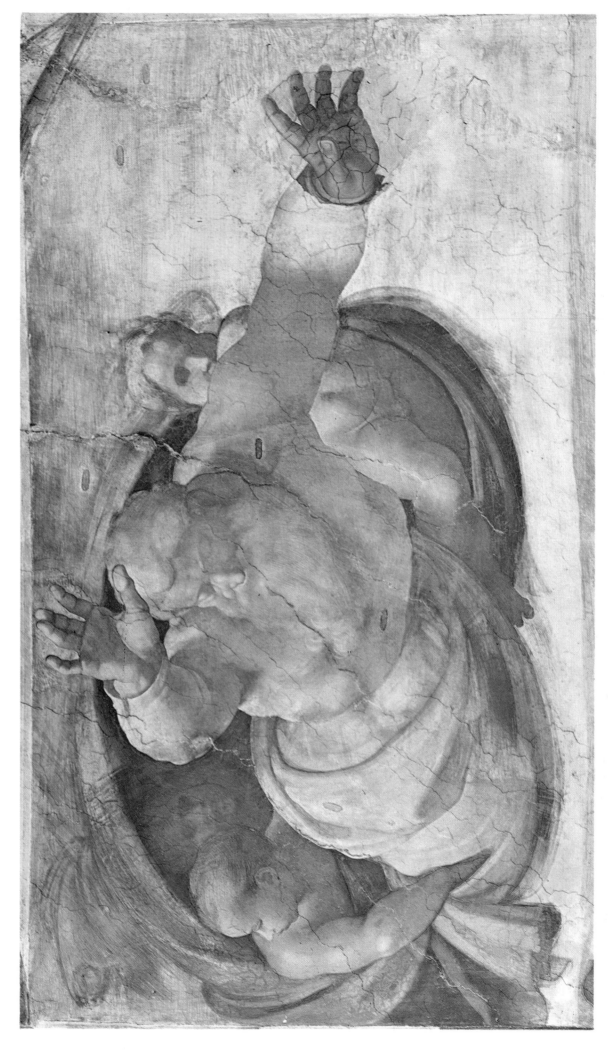

19. *THE DIVISION OF LAND AND WATER*. Detail of the vault. 1510–12. Rome, Sistine Chapel

20. *THE CREATION OF ADAM.* Detail of the vault. 1510–12. Rome, Sistine Chapel

21. *THE CREATION OF ADAM.* Detail of Plate 20

22. *THE DELUGE.* Detail of the vault. 1508–10. Rome, Sistine Chapel

23. *THE DRUNKENNESS OF NOAH*. Detail of the vault. 1508–10. Rome, Sistine Chapel

24. *THE ERYTHREAN SIBYL*. Detail of the vault. 1508–10. Rome, Sistine Chapel

25. *THE PROPHET JOEL*. Detail of the vault. 1508–10. Rome, Sistine Chapel

26. *THE LAST JUDGEMENT*. Fresco 1536–41. Rome, Vatican Palace, Altar Wall of the Sistine Chapel

27. *ST. BARTHOLOMEW*. Detail of Plate 26

28. *THE CONVERSION OF ST. PAUL.* Detail of Plate 33a. Fresco. 1542–5. Rome, Vatican Palace, Pauline Chapel

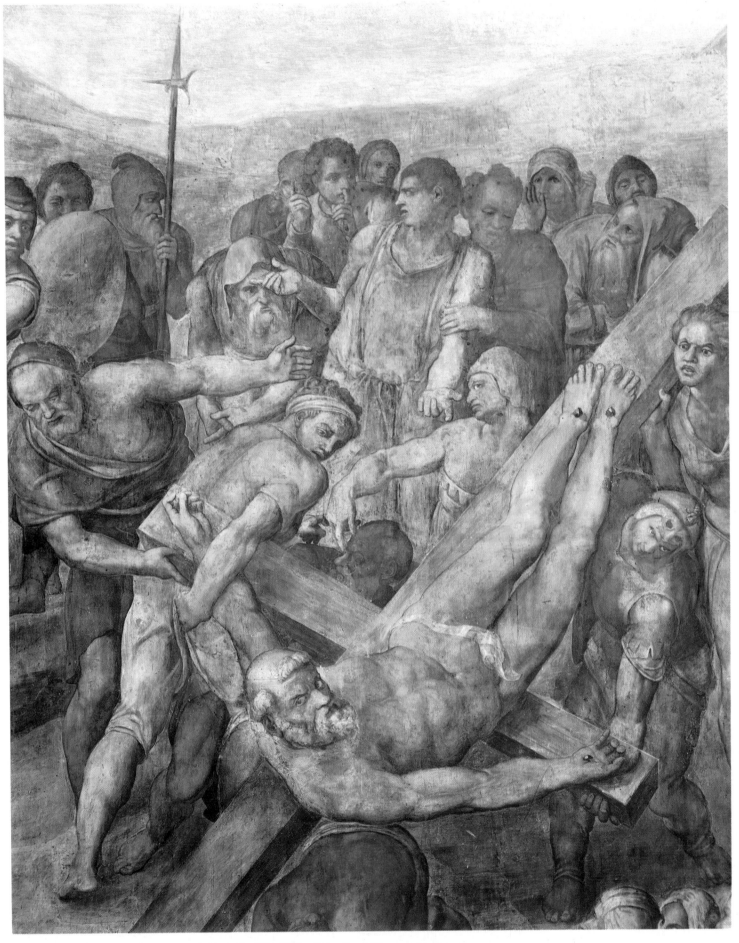

29. *THE CRUCIFIXION OF ST. PETER.* Detail of Plate 33b. Fresco. 1545–50.
Rome, Vatican Palace, Pauline Chapel

30. *THE CRUCIFIXION OF ST. PETER.* Detail of Plate 33b

31. *THE CONVERSION OF ST. PAUL.* Detail of Plate 33a

32. *THE CONVERSION OF ST. PAUL.* Detail of Plate 33a

33a. *THE CONVERSION OF ST. PAUL*. Fresco. 1542–5.
Rome, Vatican Palace, Pauline Chapel

33b. *THE CRUCIFIXION OF ST. PETER*. Fresco. 1545–50.
Rome, Vatican Palace, Pauline Chapel

34. *TOMB OF LORENZO DE'MEDICI.* Marble. 1524–33. Florence. S. Lorenzo, New Sacristy

35. *TOMB OF GIULIANO DE'MEDICI*. Marble. 1524–33. Florence, S. Lorenzo, New Sacristy

36. *LORENZO DE' MEDICI.* Detail of Plate 34

37. *GIULIANO DE'MEDICI*. Detail of Plate 35

38. '*TWILIGHT*'. Detail of Plate 34

39. '*DAWN*'. Detail of Plate 34

40. *OWL*. Detail of Plate 35

41. *MADONNA AND CHILD* (The Medici Madonna). Marble. 1524–33. Florence, S. Lorenzo, New Sacristy

42. *VICTORY*. Marble. Perhaps 1530. Florence, Palazzo Vecchio

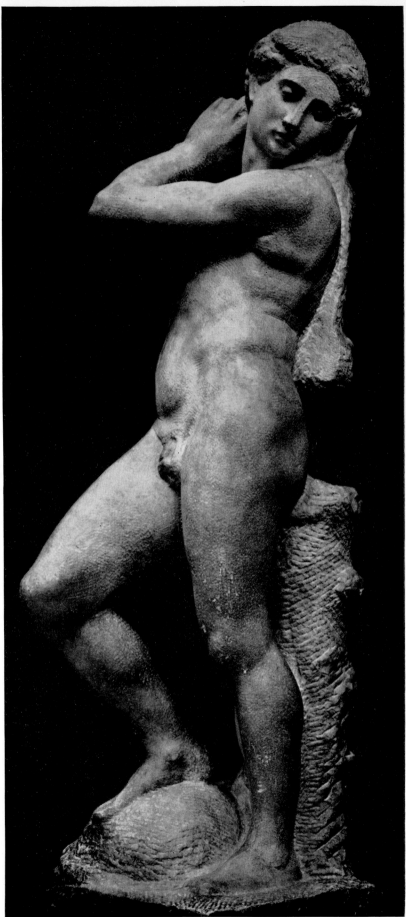

43. *DAVID – APOLLO*. Marble. 1531. Florence, Museo Nazionale del Bargello

44. *BRUTUS*. Marble. 1542–5. Florence, Museo Nazionale del Bargello

45. *HEAD OF THE 'BEARDED CAPTIVE'*. Marble. 1518–26. Florence, Accademia

46. *THE DEPOSITION FROM THE CROSS.* Marble. 1548–56. Florence, Duomo

47. *HEAD OF NICODEMUS*. Detail of Plate 46

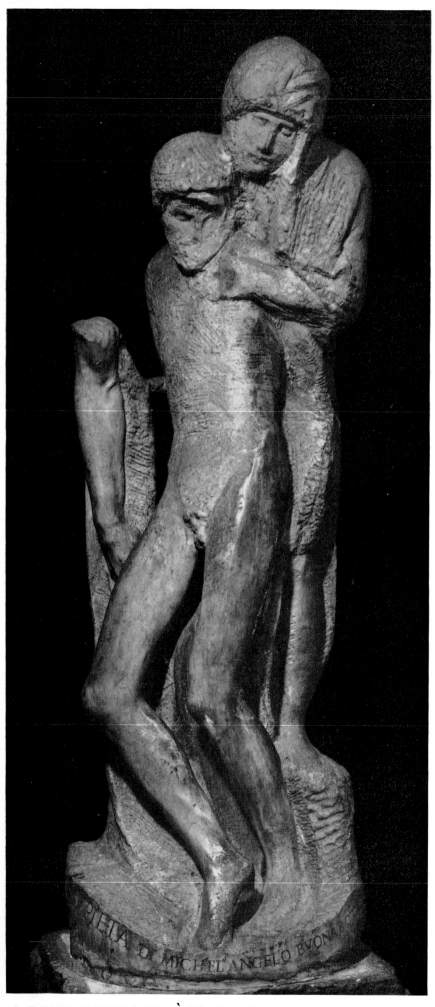

48. *RONDANINI PIETÀ*. Marble. 1556–64. Milan, Castello Sforzesco